About the Book

This is an interactive book designed to introduce young children (ages 3-6) to the Tamil alphabet through the lens of food. This unique approach blends language learning with the vibrant world of Tamil cuisine, offering children a fun and memorable way to discover the beauty of Tamil vowels while exploring iconic South indian dishes.

Each page features a Tamil food item, each corresponding to one of the 12 vowels in the Tamil alphabet. With vivid illustrations and simple explanations, children will not only learn the sounds and pronunciation of Tamil vowels but also get a taste of Tamil culture through food. From idli to sambar, Aappam to Opputu, the book brings together language, tradition, and art in a way that's both educational and entertaining.

அ

அன்னம்

அ

ஆப்பம்

இட்லி

ஈச்சம்பழ அல்வா

2

உப்புமா

ஊத்தப்பம்

எள்ளு சாதம்

ஏலக்காய் தேநீர்

ஐந்தரிசி பணியாரம்

ஒப்புட்டு

ஓமக்களி

ஒள

ஔனம்

www.ingramcontent.com/pod-product-compliance
Lightning Source LLC
LaVergne TN
LVHW071344071026
849580LV00002BA/890
* 9 7 9 8 3 4 9 2 7 1 3 5 9 *